My Alpaca is a Jerk

My Alpaca is a Jerk

(But We Love Him)

Kristen Hill

gatekeeper press
Columbus, OH

This book is a work of fiction. The names, characters and events in this book are the products of the author's imagination or are used fictitiously. Any similarity to real persons living or dead is coincidental and not intended by the author.

The views and opinions expressed in this book are solely those of the author and do not reflect the views or opinions of Gatekeeper Press. Gatekeeper Press is not to be held responsible for and expressly disclaims responsibility of the content herein.

My Alpaca is a Jerk: (But We Love Him)
Published by Gatekeeper Press
2167 Stringtown Rd, Suite 109
Columbus, OH 43123-2989
www.GatekeeperPress.com

Copyright © 2021 by Kristen Hill
All rights reserved. Neither this book, nor any parts within it may be sold or reproduced in any form or by any electronic or mechanical means, including information storage and retrieval systems, without permission in writing from the author. The only exception is by a reviewer, who may quote short excerpts in a review.

The cover design, interior formatting, typesetting, and editorial work for this book are entirely the product of the author. Gatekeeper Press did not participate in and is not responsible for any aspect of these elements.

Library of Congress Control Number: 2021947086

ISBN (hardcover): 9781662919985
ISBN (paperback): 9781662919992
eISBN: 9781662920004

I dedicate this book to my husband Brian who continues to support me in all my animal adventures and is in full support of my sense of humor.

To my three amazing kids: Jessica, Paige, and Carson. They motivate me to be the best mama to not only them, but to all of my animals. Thank you for putting up with your high maintenance mother.

It was a sunny day.
The weather was hot.
And there was my alpaca,
Sir Spits A Lot.

We love the outside,
fresh air, and the breeze.
But something was wrong.
We smelled vomit and cheese.

He spits when he is happy.
He spits when he is sad.
He spits when he is excited.
He spits when he is mad.

He stares you down with a look of such surprise.

His nose will begin to twitch. His eyes will have a glare.

The next thing you know, you have spit in your hair.

We cleaned up Nana with a warm wet rag.
When she smelled his juicy spit, she started to gag.

Now, now, Nana. He does not mean to be such a shit.
Sir Spits A Lot just likes to say hello with a mouthful of spit.

Her eyes were watering.
They began to sting.
She was so damn mad.
She wanted to kick him in the ding.

We tried to scold him.
We tried to be nice.
But he was being an asshole,
so we had to think twice.

Oh dear Sir Spits A Lot.
Why are you so grumpy?
Can't you be gentle?
Be kind and not so jumpy?

So, we all forgave his turd-like behavior.
We gave him a hug and asked for a favor.

Hello my friends- I'm Kristen. I am a mama to 3 humans, wife to 1 and animal mama to 3 alpacas, 4 pot belly pigs, 1 hedgehog, 3 cats and 1 little dog. When I am not selling "technology stuff" during my day job, I am usually outside with my hobby farm in the Pacific Northwest scooping up poop and loving my animals. My sense of humor is a big part of almost every day in the life at the hobby farm. I enjoy capturing real life situations (even the gross ones) and turning them into something fun I can share, like this book. My goal is to make you laugh and bring a smile to your day.

I am a huge supporter for animals and specifically for pigs and alpacas. There are many wonderful sanctuaries that save animals in Washington, and I encourage you to check some out.
*Olympic Peninsula Llama/Alpaca Rescue Non-Profit
Port Angeles WA
*Heartwood Haven Non-Profit
Gig Harbor WA

www.ingramcontent.com/pod-product-compliance
Lightning Source LLC
LaVergne TN
LVHW071733060526
838200LV00031B/484